X-RAY
AF428346

Book layout by Kayla Meadows Design
www.kaylameadows.com

ISBN
979-8-89217-652-1 (Paperback)
979-8-89217-653-8 (Hard Cover)

TEDDY
VISITS THE VET

Written By Christine Milkovic Krauss

Illustrated by Cierra Van Nes

Get ready Teddy!
It's time to visit the Vet!

A Veterinarian is a doctor
for all kinds of pets!

A Vet can help animals
that are sick or injured and
ensure they stay healthy with
simple, routine check ups.

A F C H L
B Q T I
M O R Z S U L
P T L Q D E V R A
O N I B G J P K E L O V
Just like us when
we visit a Doctor
or a Dentist!

Teddy needs extra medical care as he had many injuries from living his life completely outdoors.

Teddy has never been to a doctor or a dentist before.

This is his first visit!

RECE

WATER

The Doctor needs to examine him.
Teddy is nervous because he doesn't know what to expect.
If you ever feel anxious about your visit to the Doctor, ask any questions you have to a trusted adult before you go!

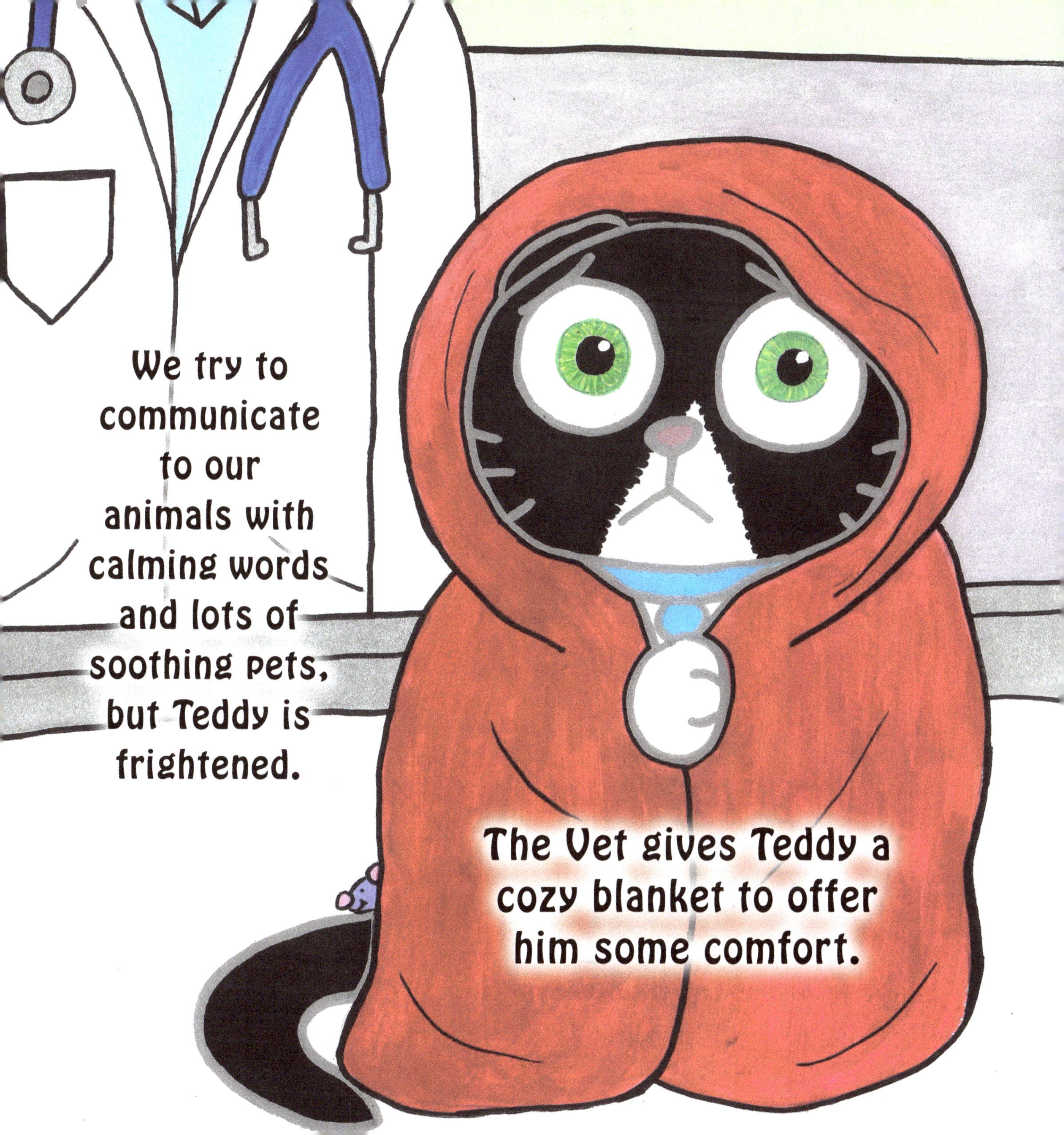

We try to communicate to our animals with calming words and lots of soothing pets, but Teddy is frightened.
The Vet gives Teddy a cozy blanket to offer him some comfort.

...Inhale...2...3...4... Exhale...
Sometimes when we feel scared, it can be beneficial to close your eyes and take slow deep breaths.

When we learn to focus our attention on breathing consciously, it can reduce anxiety and help us calm our body.

HAPPY EASTER
Heart & Soul
Dog & Cat Rescue Society
Animal: Cat
Gender: Male
Age: 3 y/o
Diagnosis:
Frostbite Injuries
Before Teddy was adopted on Easter Day, there was little known information available to his guardians about his life and where he came from.

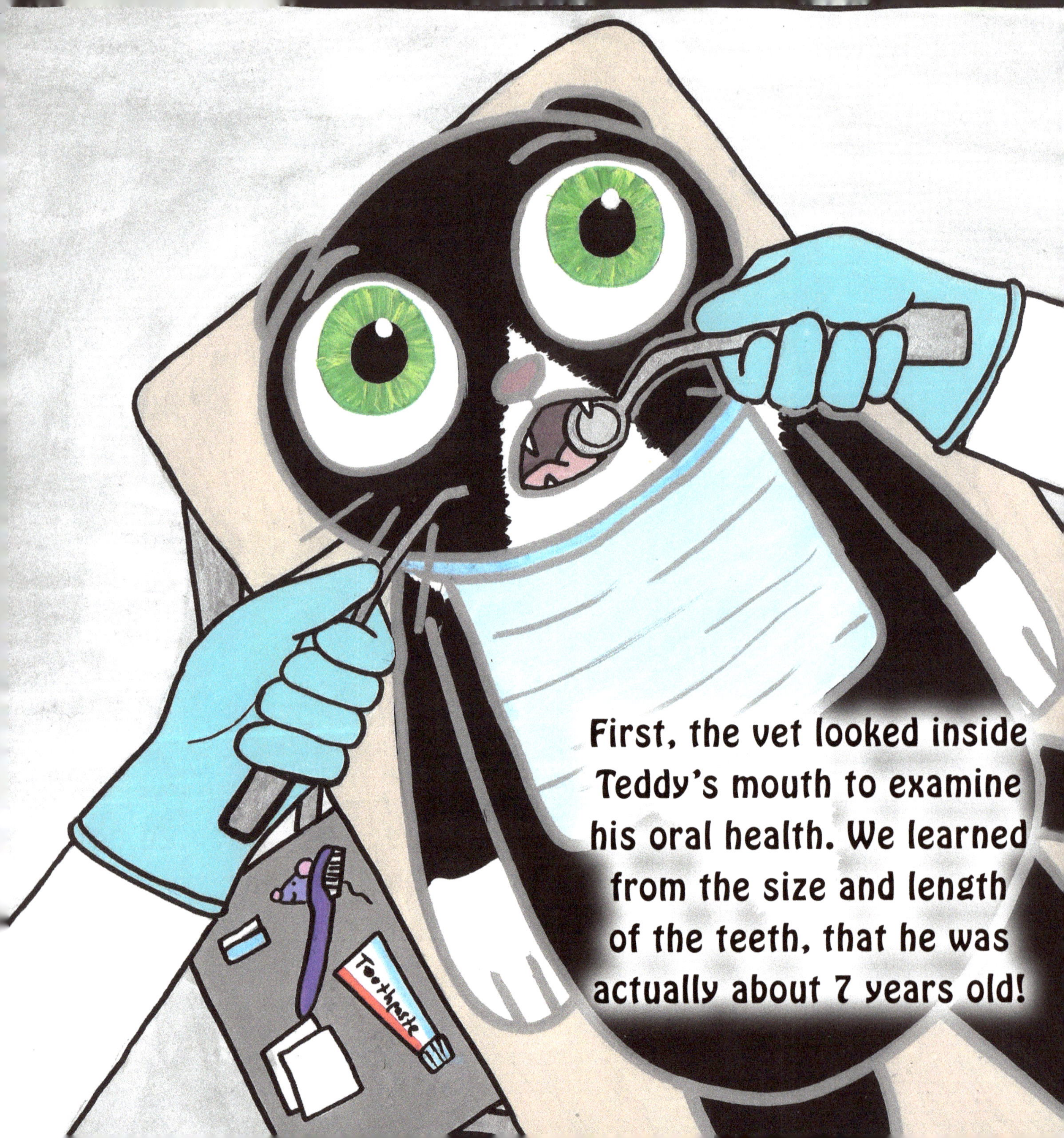
First, the vet looked inside Teddy's mouth to examine his oral health. We learned from the size and length of the teeth, that he was actually about 7 years old!

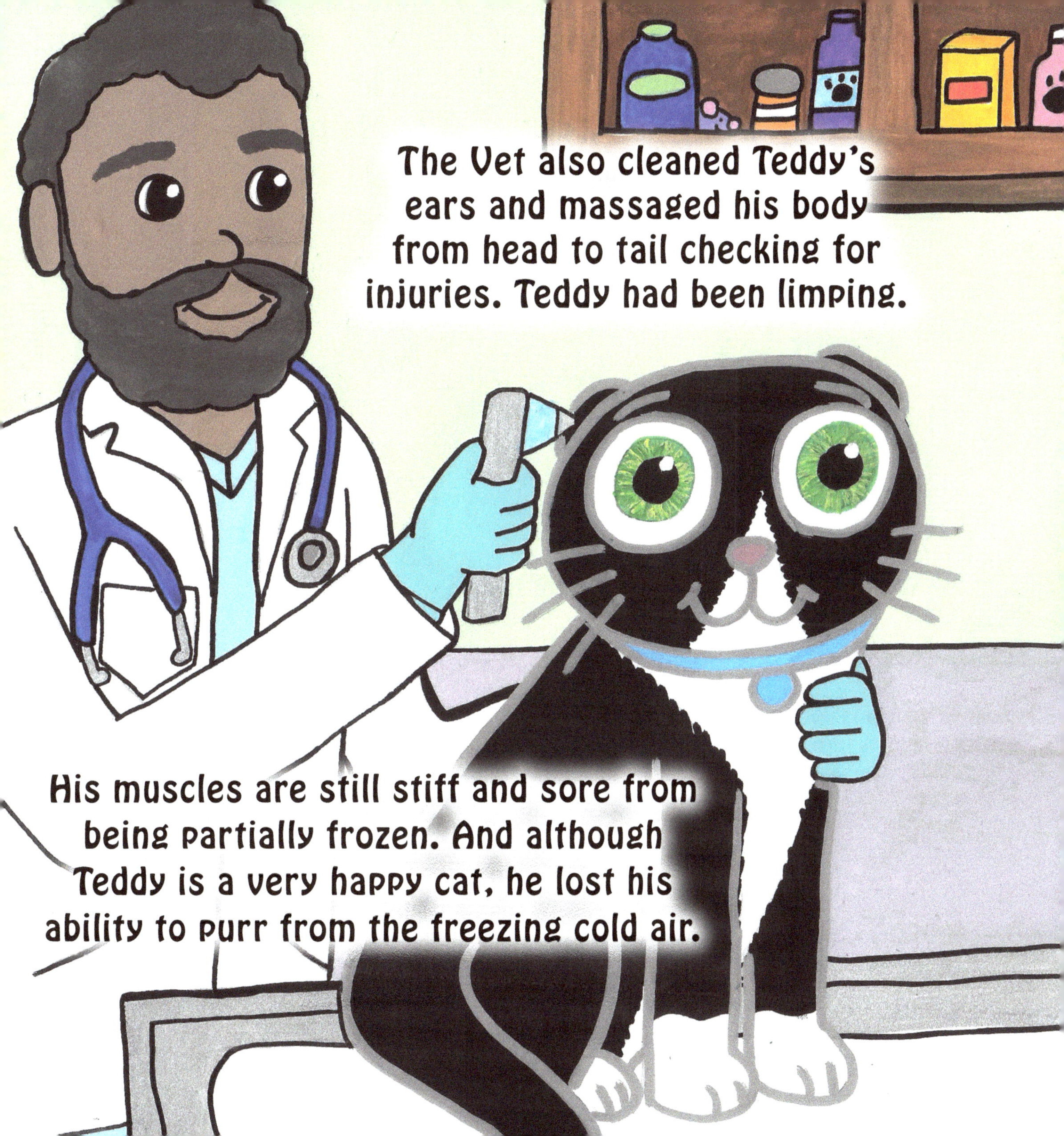
The Vet also cleaned Teddy's ears and massaged his body from head to tail checking for injuries. Teddy had been limping.
His muscles are still stiff and sore from being partially frozen. And although Teddy is a very happy cat, he lost his ability to purr from the freezing cold air.

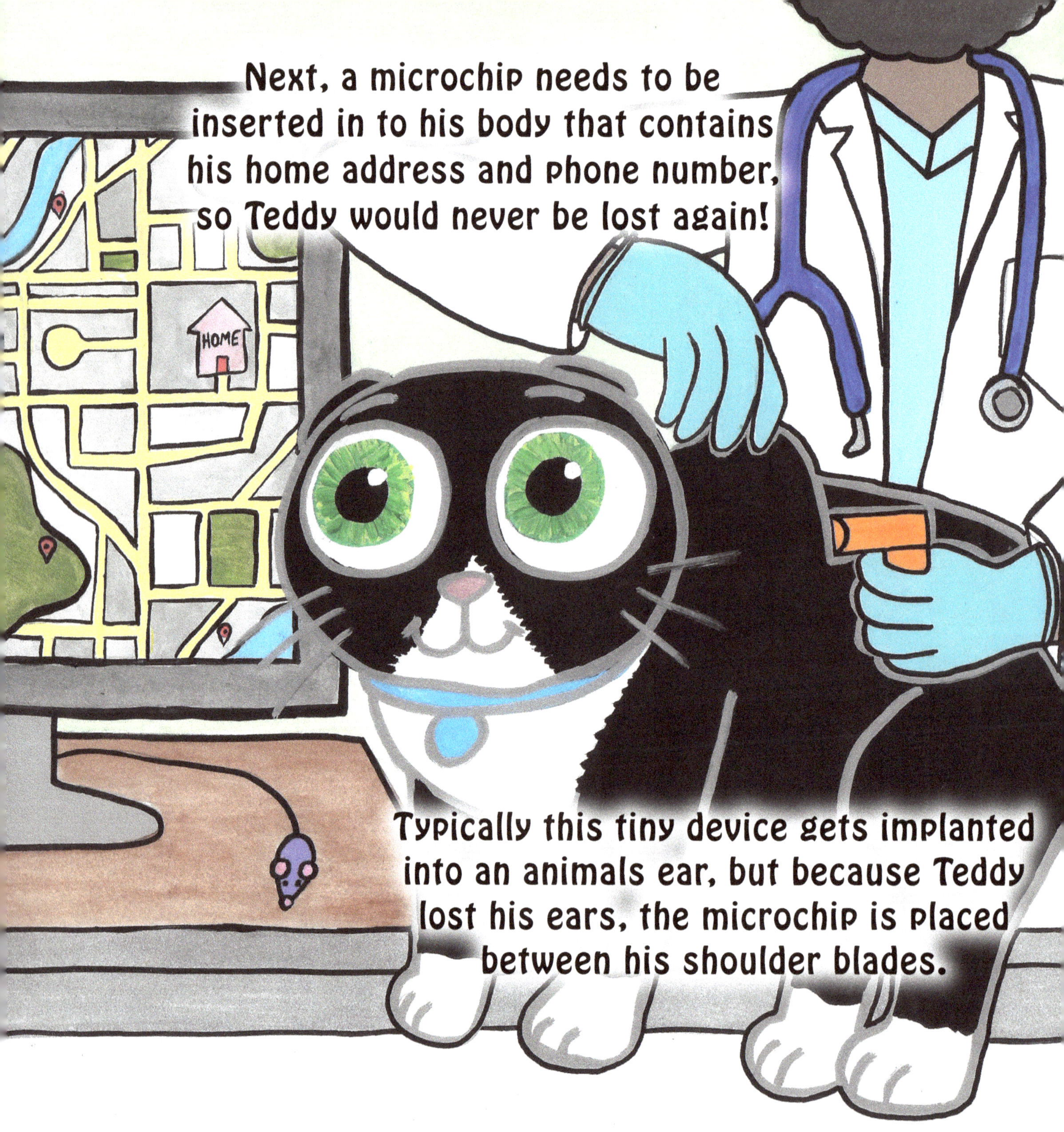
Next, a microchip needs to be inserted in to his body that contains his home address and phone number, so Teddy would never be lost again!

HOME

Typically this tiny device gets implanted into an animals ear, but because Teddy lost his ears, the microchip is placed between his shoulder blades.

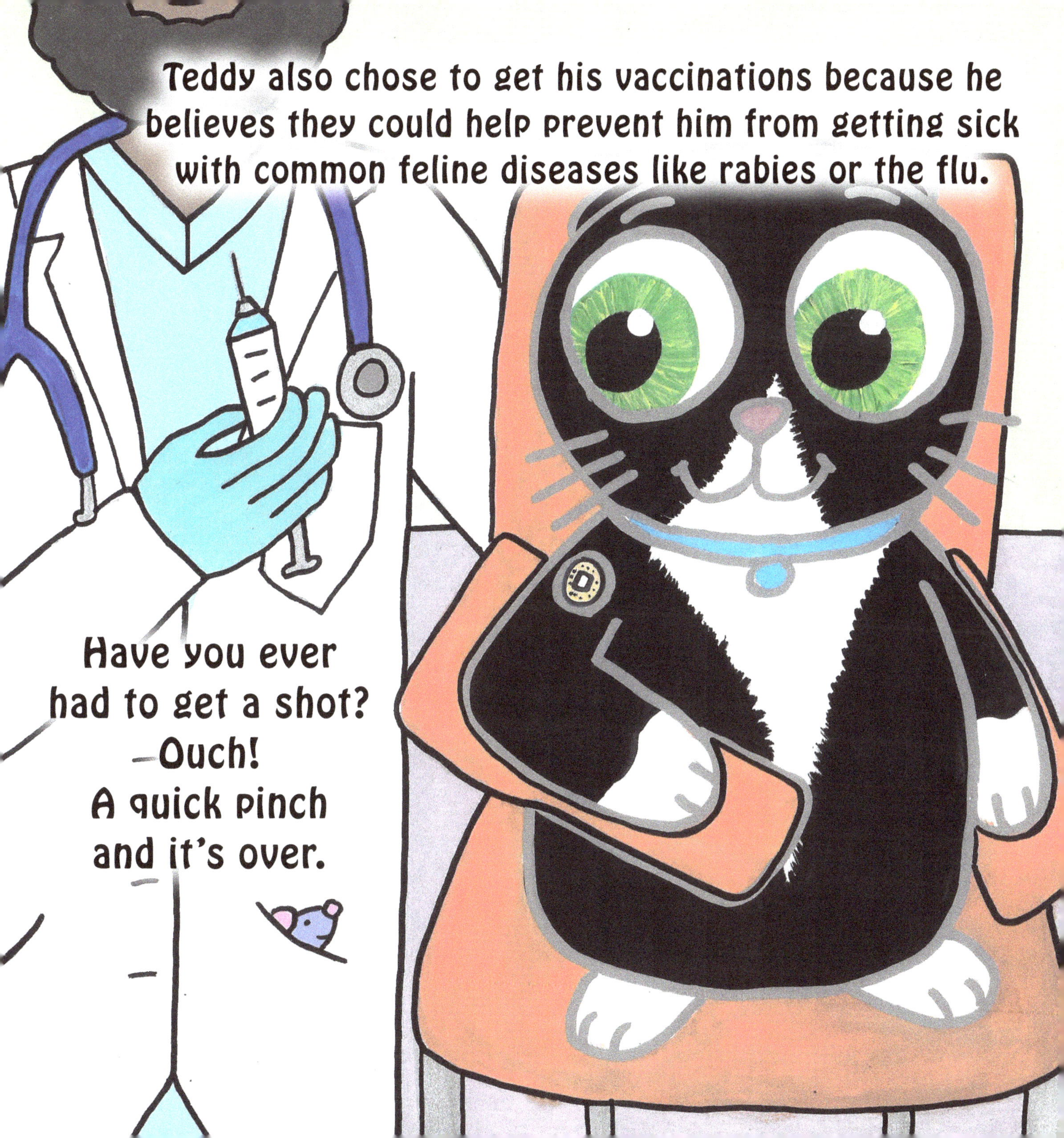

Teddy also chose to get his vaccinations because he believes they could help prevent him from getting sick with common feline diseases like rabies or the flu.

Have you ever had to get a shot? —Ouch! A quick pinch and it's over.

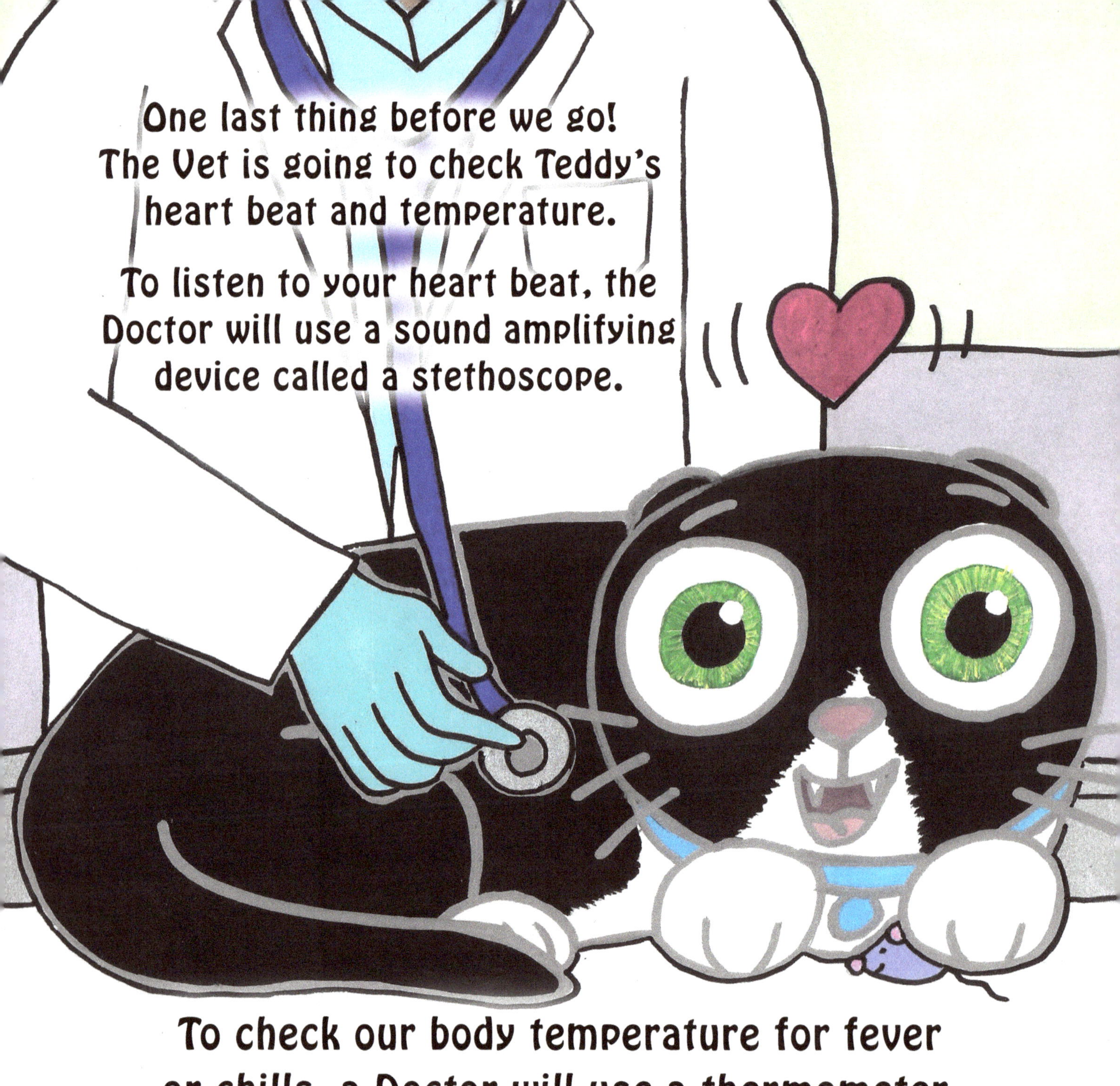

One last thing before we go!
The Vet is going to check Teddy's
heart beat and temperature.

To listen to your heart beat, the
Doctor will use a sound amplifying
device called a stethoscope.

To check our body temperature for fever
or chills, a Doctor will use a thermometer.

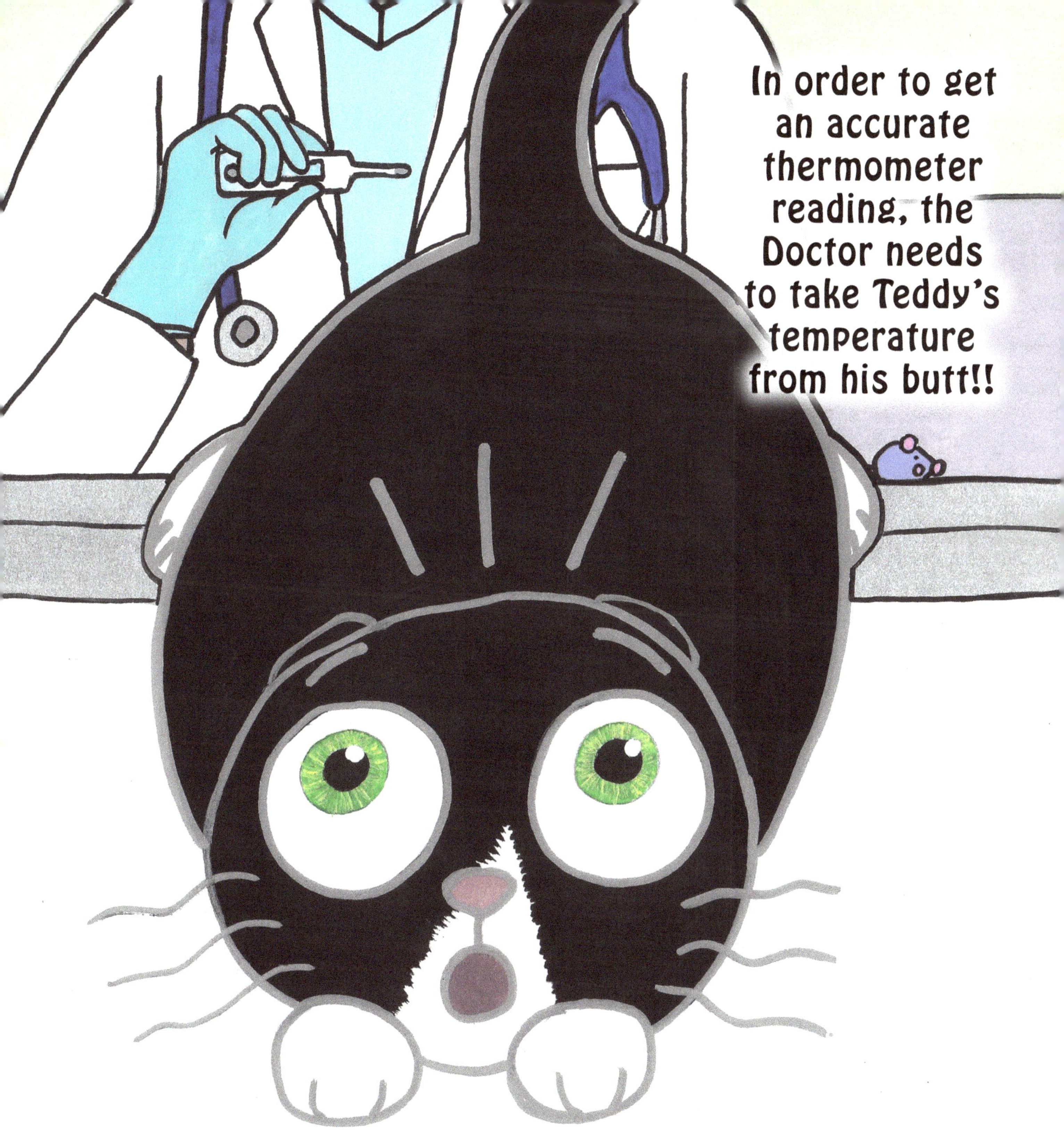

In order to get an accurate thermometer reading, the Doctor needs to take Teddy's temperature from his butt!!

Hmmmm...this paperwork
says Teddy is a male.
?
This cat is
not a male!!!

Mew!
Teddy is a FEMALE?!?!?

The children had a better idea. They wanted to give Teddy the opportunity to decide which collar they would like to choose for themselves!

People have often made assumptions about Teddy.

Friendly

Those who took the time to know the real Teddy, discovered them to be:

Affectionate

Nurturing

Grateful

Playful

Mysterious

Compassionate

Considerate

Sweet and Petite

Teddy was all of these things and more!

She was also proud be known as a courageous, fierce, intelligent, strong, dynamic, and powerful GIRL!

Teddy never really cared what people thought about her anyway. Their opinions would not stop her from being her genuine self.

Teddy is inclusive and kind and promotes love for all pets and people.

Teddy studied her options.

Although Teddy identified with the pink collar, she
made a choice to celebrate all of her beautiful colours!

SNAP!
The family was supportive of Teddy's choice and felt proud to snap that new rainbow collar around her neck!

Teddy was living her truth. Whatever Teddy would have decided, she knew she was loved by everyone who knew her.

She knows exactly who she is!

RAINBOW TEDDY

  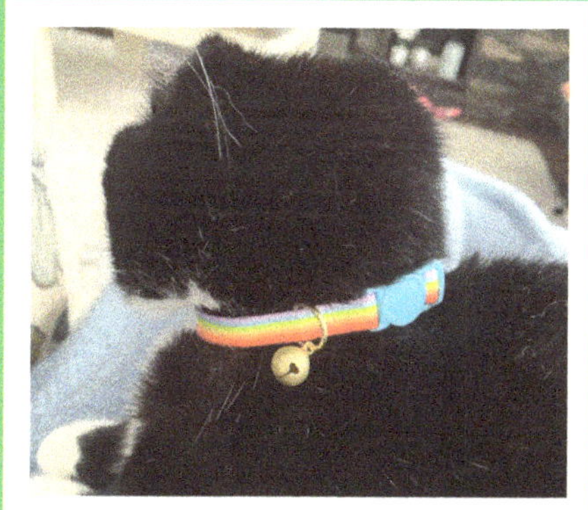

Teddy sincerely hopes by sharing her stories, that friends have grown to know who she truly is and have learned that kindness can change someone's life. There are many animals in need of rescue or temporary foster and you can be a helper too!
For more photos of Teddy at home,
scan the QR code below.